HIP-HOP & R&B

Culture, Music & Storytelling

Cardi B

HIP-HOP & R&B

Culture, Music & Storytelling

MASON CREST
Joe L. Morgan

HIP-HOP & R&B
Cardi B

Culture, Music & Storytelling

Mason Crest
450 Parkway Drive, Suite D
Broomall, Pennsylvania 19008
(866) MCP-BOOK (toll free)

First printing
9 8 7 6 5 4 3 2 1

hardback: 978-1-4222-4186-8
series: 978-1-4222-4176-9
ebook: 978-1-4222-7628-0

Library of Congress Cataloging-in-Publication Data

Names: Morgan, Joe L. author
Title: Cardi B / Joe L. Morgan.
Description: Broomall, PA : Mason Crest, 2018. | Series: Hip-hop & R&B: culture, music & storytelling.
Identifiers: LCCN 2018020767 (print) | LCCN 2018021051 (ebook) | ISBN 9781422276280 (eBook) | ISBN 9781422241868 (hardback) | ISBN 9781422241769 (series)
Subjects: LCSH: Cardi B, 1992---Juvenile literature. | Rap musicians--United States--Biography--Juvenile literature.
Classification: LCC ML3930.C255 (ebook) | LCC ML3930.C255 M67 2018 (print) | DDC 782.421649092 [B] --dc23
LC record available at https://lccn.loc.gov/2018020767

Developed and Produced by National Highlights, Inc.
Editor: Susan Uttendorfsky
Interior and cover design: Annalisa Gumbrecht, Studio Gumbrecht
Production: Michelle Luke

QR CODES AND LINKS TO THIRD-PARTY CONTENT

CONTENTS

KEY ICONS TO LOOK FOR:

 Words to understand: These words with their easy-to-understand definitions will increase the reader's understanding of the text while building vocabulary skills.

 Sidebars: This boxed material within the main text allows readers to build knowledge, gain insights, explore possibilities, and broaden their perspectives by weaving together additional information to provide realistic and holistic perspectives.

 Educational videos: Readers can view videos by scanning our QR codes, providing them with additional educational content to supplement the text. Examples include news coverage, moments in history, speeches, iconic sports moments, and much more!

 Text-dependent questions: These questions send the reader back to the text for more careful attention to the evidence presented there.

 Research projects: Readers are pointed toward areas of further inquiry connected to each chapter. Suggestions are provided for projects that encourage deeper research and analysis.

 Series of glossary of key terms: This back-of-the-book glossary contains terminology used throughout this series. Words found here increase the reader's ability to read and comprehend higher-level books and articles in this field.

Cardi B
HIP-HOP & R&B

Chapter 1

Cardi B's Highlights Reel

Cardi B may never have thought that in her life she would go from humble beginnings growing up in the Bronx, New York—born of a mother from Trinidad and a father from the Dominican Republic—to working in a lower Manhattan supermarket to reality star and top female rapper. She certainly would have never counted on such success coming her way all before the young age of twenty-five.

Cardi B has used her reality show stardom and an independent spirit to become a noticeable rising hip-hop and rap star. She has already put out several albums and mixtapes, singles, and collaborations with many industry stars, such as Bruno Mars, and is worth paying attention to as someone who is taking the industry by storm.

Cardi B's music is a true reflection of who she is and what she has become in these few number of years. The realness of her sound and message has a broad

appeal and she has picked up fans from all over the globe. She challenges traditional boundaries and puts up beats that are soul rattling, challenging, entertaining, and powerful.

Cardi B's Playlist

Mixtapes

GBM, Vol. 1

(Released March 07, 2016)

Cardi B released her debut mixtape, GBM, Vol. 1, at the age of twenty-four while she was a member of the cast of VH1's reality TV show, *Love & Hip Hop: New York*. The thirteen-song mixtape, produced by KSR Group, was released on Apple Music, as well as through digital music download platforms SoundCloud and DatPiff.com. The mixtape was liked more than 139,000 times on SoundCloud and downloaded the same number of times from DatPiff.com. The production has also been listened to more than 744,000 times on DatPiff.com.

COLLABORATIONS

- *Intro (Skit)*, featuring Breakfast Club
- *Selfish*, featuring Josh X
- *Trick (Skit)*, featuring Haitian V
- *Outro (Skit)*, featuring Lisa Evers

Scan the code here to listen to *Trick*, one of the first tracks appearing on Cardi B's debut mixtape, GBM, Vol. 1

UNDERESTIMATED: THE ALBUM
(Released September 12, 2016)

The second release from Cardi B, UNDERESTIMATED: THE ALBUM, was a collaborative mixtape of various KSR Group musicians who participated in an eleven-city tour in 2016. The artists included HoodCelebrityy, SwiftOnDemand, Cashflow Harlem, and Josh X, and featured different music genres. Cardi B contributed three solo tracks and collaborated on another three singles. Her partnership with Josh X on the single *Heaven on My Mind* peaked at number twenty-two on *Billboard's* Hot 100 Chart on January 21, 2017. The popular track stayed on the charts for an amazing twenty weeks.

COLLABORATIONS

- *Want My Love Back,* featuring Cashflow Harlem
- *Island Girls*, featuring HoodCelebrityy and Josh X
- *Heaven on My Mind*, featuring Josh X

GBM, VOL. 2
(Released January 20, 2017)

Cardi B's third mixtape was released on January 20, 2017, again by her label KSR Group, for digital download. The production reached number twenty-five on *Billboard's* Independent Album Chart, two spots higher than her first

Scan the code to watch the video for *Heaven on My Mind*, a song that was performed by Cardi B during her headlining UNDERESTIMATED: THE ALBUM

release, GBM, Vᴏʟ. 1. That mixtape peaked at number twenty-seven on the same chart. Tʜᴇ Vᴏʟ. 2 release included ten singles and has been downloaded nearly 23,000 times and listened to 215,000 times on DatPiff.com. SoundCloud users have liked the mixtape 9,790 times.

COLLABORATIONS

- *Lick,* featuring Offset
- *Hectic,* featuring DJ Hardwerk
- *Leave That _____ Alone (Skit),* featuring Justvlad
- *Back It Up,* featuring Konshens and Hoodcelebrityy
- *Never Give Up*, featuring Josh X
- *Pop Off,* featuring Casanova

Stand-Alone Singles

In addition to the three mixtapes to her credit, Cardi B has released six solo singles. Her biggest offering to date, *Bodak Yellow (Money Moves)*, soared to the top of the charts, becoming the first rap song to hit number one on *Billboard's* Hot 100 Chart in two decades.

Cheap _____ Weave (Released December 25, 2015)

This earliest single release by Cardi B was made available by digital download.

Scan this code to listen to *Never Give Up*, a single from Cardi B's third mixtape, GBM, Vᴏʟ. 2, released January 20, 2017

Str_____per H_____
(Released February 15, 2016)

This effort marked her breakout from her appearances on VH1's *Love & Hip Hop: New York*, her launch pad to the music scene. The song was made available for free as a digital download.

Album Singles

What a Girl Likes
(Released July 18, 2016)

What a Girl Likes was part of the album UNDERESTIMATED: THE ALBUM, a collaborative production of the artists of KSR Group. They participated in an eleven-city music tour, headlined by Cardi B, in July 2016. The track was written by Cardi B and released digitally through iTunes and other digital platform outlets as part of the tour's promotion.

Nawlage and Cardi B

Bronx Season
(Released September 15, 2016)

This single was made available by Cardi B on the digital platform iTunes and others in September 2016. *Bronx Season* was on her third mixtape, GBM, Vol. 2, which was released in February of 2017.

Bodak Yellow
(Money Moves)
(Released June 16, 2017)

Cardi B cemented her name in the books as one to watch with the June 16, 2017, release of the song *Bodak Yellow (Money Moves)*. The track made history as the second rap song to reach the number one position on the *Billboard* Hot 100 Chart. The last time was Lauryn Hill, with her megahit release of *Doo-Wop (That Thing)* in November 1998.

The song also reached number six on Canada's Hot 100, as well as number one on *Billboard*'s Rhythmic Songs and Hot R&B/Hip-Hop Songs charts. The production was Cardi B's debut single through a major

Lauryn Hill

recording studio, Atlantic Records, and was initially made available as a digital download. Later, on August 01, 2017, it was released as an urban contemporary entry for R&B and hip-hop radio playlists across the United States.

The song has been certified by the RIAA (Recording Industry Association of America) as triple Platinum, by Australia's ARIA (Australian Recording Industry Association) as a Gold song, by the UK's BPI (British Phonographic Industry) as a Silver hit, by Music Canada as double Platinum, and by New Zealand's RMNZ (Recorded Music New Zealand, or NZ) as a certified Gold record.

Bartier Cardi, featuring 21 Savage
(Released December 22, 2017)

Bartier Cardi is Cardi B's second single release through her deal with Atlantic Records and is scheduled to be included in her upcoming debut studio album, as yet unnamed. The single was made available December 22, 2017, and is her third single to appear in the top twenty of *Billboard*'s Hot 100. This includes her major recording label debut single *Bodak Yellow (Money Moves)*, which made it to number one, and a collaboration with Migos and Nicki Minaj on the song *MotorSports*. That song peaked at number fourteen on the *Billboard* Hot 100 Chart.

Scan the code to watch *Bodak Yellow (Money Moves)*, which became the first hip-hop song to reach the *Billboard* Hot 100 since Lauryn Hill's 1998 *Doo-Wop (That Thing)* topped the chart

Scan the code to listen to *Bartier Cardi*, which features Atlanta-based rapper 21 Savage and is the follow-up hit to Cardi B's number one smash, *Bodak Yellow (Money Moves)*

Tours, Award Shows, and Other Performances

Cardi B and Friends Tour

Cardi B's first career tour began in July 2016 as part of the promotion of KSR Group's up-and-coming artists. The monthlong schedule kicked off on July 01 at the TAO Event Center venue in Portland, Oregon. Then there were stops in Atlanta, Georgia; Orlando, Florida; Washington, DC; Providence, Rhode Island; and Philadelphia, Pennsylvania. They finished in front of a packed crowd at New York City's Stage 48 on July 29, 2016.

The tour was billed as "Cardi B and Friends," and the lineup featured several artists who were signed by the KSR Group at the time: Cashflow Harlem, HoodCelebrityy, Josh X, and SwiftOnDemand. The album UNDERESTIMATED: THE ALBUM was released several weeks later.

MTV Video Music Awards

Cardi B performed her number one single *Bodak Yellow (Money Moves)* at the 2017 MTV Video Music Awards. The event, which took place on August 27, was held at The Forum, located in Inglewood, California.

Power 99 Powerhouse Concert

Cardi B was part of Philadelphia's Power 99 Powerhouse Concert on October 27, 2017. Along with Migos and Nicki Minaj, Cardi B performed their Hot 100 hit *MotorSports*. During the stage show, "she received one of the best offers in her young career": a proposal of marriage from her boyfriend, Offset, who is also in the group Migos. Cardi B said yes, and her fans wildly showed their approval as she completed her concert gig.

TrapCircus Music Festival

The TrapCircus Music Festival was the next venue Cardi B performed at. The event was held at the RC Cola Plant Museum in Miami, Florida, on November 22, 2017. This show, on the eve of Thanksgiving, also featured a performance from a fellow KSR Group member— Jamaican-American rapper HoodCelebrityy.

Scan here to watch the 2016 announcement for the Cardi B and Friends performances in the eleven-city UNDERESTIMATED: THE ALBUM jaunt, from July 01–29, 2016

Scan here to watch Cardi B perform her hit single *Bodak Yellow (Money Moves)* at the 2017 MTV Video Music Awards on August 27

iHeart Radio Jingle Ball Canada

A star-studded group of entertainers—including Backstreet Boys, Fergie, Fifth Harmony, Kelly Clarkson, Noah Cyrus, and Canadian artists Jessie Reyez, Ria Mae, and Virginia to Vegas—joined Cali B in traveling to Toronto for the 2017 iHeart Radio Jingle Ball Canada. The concert was held on December 09 at the city's Air Canada Centre.

Hot 97 Hot for the Holidays Concert

Cardi B participated in the Hot 97 Hot for the Holidays Concert on December 14, 2017. She joined Chris Brown and 21 Savage, among other artists, at the Prudential Center in Newark, New Jersey. The performance capped off a busy 2017 season for the young star and placed her in a crowd with the elites in hip-hop and rap, celebrating the success of her three Hot 100–charting singles after signing with Atlantic Records.

Trap-mas Party

Following her Hot for the Holidays Concert performance, Cardi B returned to the stage

Fergie

on December 15, 2017, for a party featuring the hip-hop "trap" style of music. With Cardi B, YFN Lucci, Dave East, and Young Ma, the event took place at The Grand Theater at the Foxwoods Resort Casino in Mashantucket, Connecticut.

Schedule for 2018

Cardi B is set to perform with Bruno Mars on their collaboration hit, *Finesse (Remix),* at the 60th Grammy Awards on January 28, 2018, to kick off her 2018 performance schedule. This appearance leads to a much-anticipated gig at the Coachella Music Festival Weekend, April 13–15, in Indio, California. Then it's off to a joint show with rapper Lil Wayne on May 03 at the Broadbent Arena in Louisville, Kentucky.

Other 2018 performances that Cardi B has committed to include a concert with DJ Holiday on February 01 at Privé Minneapolis, a live music venue in Minnesota. She also has a date to perform at RFK Stadium in Washington, DC, on April 28, 2018. Scheduled to join her onstage are Nipsey Hussle, Miguel, Lightshow, Daniel Caesar, Migos, Rich the Kid, and Grits and Biscuits.

Bruno Mars

Collaborating with Other Artists

Cardi B is credited on thirteen collaborative musical works from 2015–2018.

Boom Boom (Remix) by Shaggy, featuring Cardi B and Popcaan
(Released November 25, 2015)

Shaggy

The song *Boom Boom (Remix)* is one of Cardi B's earliest collaborative efforts. She is a featured artist on this remix of a July 2015 song by singer Shaggy, along with Jamaican deejay Popcaan. The track is listed as a dance hall hit and, since its release, has been liked 627,000 times on the digital download site SoundCloud.

Gimme _____ Too by J.R., featuring Cardi B
(Released August 31, 2016)

Cardi B partnered with rapper J.R. (Junior) on this single, which appeared on his album IN DUE TIME. On the digital download platform SoundCloud, the track has been liked 3,035 times.

_____ Me Up by TJR, featuring Cardi B
(Released June 06, 2016)

The young hip-hop artist teamed up with American deejay and Melbourne bounce producer Thomas Joseph "TJR" Rozdilsky on his single _____ *Me Up*. Spinnin' Records produced the track. The digital download was made available through SoundCloud and has been listened to on that platform more than 1.03 million times.

Want My Love Back by Cashflow Harlem, featuring Cardi B and Ryan Dudley
(Released June 27, 2016)

Cardi B went to work with artist Cashflow Harlem and Ryan Dudley on Cashflow Harlem's *Want My Love Back*. The mixtape the track appears on, RICH THOUGHTS POOR HABITS, can be downloaded from DatPiff.com. The collaboration single itself has more than 15,400 downloads.

Island Girls by HoodCelebrityy, featuring Cardi B, Josh X, and Young Chow
(Released June 28, 2016)

Island Girls was a collaborative work between Cardi B and fellow KSR Group members HoodCelebrityy, Josh X, and Young Chow. The song was an extended play (EP) release for digital download on the mixtape UNDERESTIMATED: THE ALBUM. The mixtape has been listened to more than 474,000 times on DatPiff.com and has over 26,000 downloads.

She a Bad One (BBA) (Remix) by Red Café, featuring Cardi B
(Released July 22, 2016)

The KSR Group released *She a Bad One (BBA) (Remix)* on July 22, 2016, near the end of Cardi B's monthlong, eleven-city tour with other KSR Group artists as part of the Cardi B and Friends Tour.

Cute (Remix) by D.R.A.M., featuring Cardi B
(Released July 27, 2017)

Bronx rapper D.R.A.M. took the opportunity to remix a digital single he had released a year prior and brought in Cardi B to help him with the vocals. The result was their collaboration *Cute (Remix)*.

D.R.A.M.

Right Now by Phresher, featuring Cardi B
(Released August 11, 2017)

Brooklyn rapper Phresher got together with Cardi B for his digital song *Right Now*. The track was made public during Cardi B's success with her number one single *Bodak Yellow (Money Moves)*. It was still charting on the Hot 100 at the time of Right Now's release, which debuted at number three.

No Limit by G-Eazy, featuring Cardi B and A$AP Rocky
(Released September 08, 2017)

G-Eazy worked with A$AP Rocky and Cardi B as collaborators for this track. The song appears on G-Eazy's album THE BEAUTIFUL & DAMNED. The song is one of Cardi B's Hot 100 top-ten successes, making it to number four on the charts. For G-Eazy, it has been his biggest hit to date.

MotorSports by Migos, featuring Cardi B and Nicki Minaj
(Released October 27, 2017)

MotorSports has been one of Cardi B's top collaborations so far, achieved with the group Migos. The album CULTURE2—produced by Capitol Motown Records and made available digitally to fans—contained this hip-hop hit track. The song became certified Gold by the RIAA and Platinum by Music Canada. It was

Nicki Minaj

the third top-twenty and second top-ten Hot 100 single for Cardi B, making it to the number six position.

Kamasut _____ by Juicy J, featuring Cardi B
(Released December 02, 2017)

Artist Juicy J collaborated with Cardi B and released their song, *Kamasut _____*. It appeared on Juicy J's album, HIGHLY INTOXICATED.

La Modelo (The Model) by Ozuna, featuring Cardi B
(Released December 22, 2017)

La Modelo (The Model) is a song by Puerto Rican recording artist Ozuna that was a collaborative effort with Cardi B. The track, which Cardi B performs both in English and Spanish, appeared on the *Billboard* Hot 100 Chart at number fifty-two and made it to number three on *Billboard*'s Hot Latin Songs Chart. The song is a celebration, of sorts, of Cardi B's Caribbean and Spanish roots.

Juicy J

Finesse (Remix), by Bruno Mars, featuring Cardi B
(Released January 04, 2018)

Finesse (Remix) is Cardi B's first *Billboard* Hot 100 hit of 2018, landing at the number three spot on the chart. The song is a remake of the prior artistry of singer Bruno Mars from his album 24ᴋ Mᴀɢɪᴄ. With the growing success of Cardi B's career, the song was a feature at the 60th Grammy Awards ceremony on January 28, 2018.

Scan the code here watch the video for *La Modelo (The Model)*, a song with Ozuna that made it to number three on *Billboard*'s Hot Latin Songs Chart

Scan the code for the video from *Finesse (Remix)*, a collaborative effort and *Billboard* Hot 100 top-five hit by Bruno Mars, featuring Cardi B as guest vocals

abuela: the Spanish word for grandmother.

aspirations: what a person hopes to become or accomplish with their life through effort and hard work.

ethnicity: a person's background; a description that is often closely associated with both a person's race and country of origin.

rift: a tear, break, or point of tension in some physical item, or in the relationship of two people.

bodega: Spanish word for small grocery store.

Chapter 2

Beginning in the Bronx

Cardi B's Childhood

The Bronx, New York City, welcomed Cardi B—born as Belcalis Almanzar—on October 11, 1992. She grew up in the Highbridge neighborhood of the Bronx with a sister, Hennessy Carolina, who was born a few years later on December 22, 1995. Cardi B's parents immigrated to the United States and met in the country before the two sisters were born.

Cardi B's mother is Trinidadian and her father is Dominican. This makes Cardi B's **ethnicity** Afro-Latin-Caribbean, but she is 100 percent born and raised in the United States. Her parents split up when she was a child, and she spent time between her Highbridge home in the Bronx and Washington Heights, another area in New York City in the borough of Manhattan, with her *abuela*.

New York City block of apartment buildings

Cardi B is very discreet about her parents' background, names, and origins, other than their respective ethnicities. This privacy, however, has not extended to posted pictures of various family members in her Instagram posts, or to having her sister, Hennessey, appear with her on TV. First Hennessey was a guest on VH1's *Love & Hip Hop: New York* (see Chapter 3 for more information), then a supporting cast member during the time that Cardi B was on the show.

Cardi B grew up with **aspirations** of greatness and making lots of money. Her family wasn't poor, but they weren't well off either. The young woman worked for a time at a supermarket in Manhattan while attending classes at an alternative high school, Renaissance, located in the Bronx. The school specializes in musical theater and technology. She lost the grocery store job by age nineteen, which made it "difficult to continue her studies at the Borough of Manhattan Community College." She left school and spent time as a dancer to make

Borough of Manhattan Community College

ends meet. This brief career choice created a **rift** between Cardi B and her mother, causing her to move out of the family home in Highbridge.

Cardi B and her sister Hennessy Carolina got their names from two favorite liquors of their father: Bacardi rum and Hennessy cognac. Cardi B was named Belcalis by her parents when she was born, but was given the nickname Bacardi, or "Cardi B," as she grew older. Her sister was born near Christmas, and their father, leaving an event upon hearing the news, immediately named his newest addition "Hennessy."

Other Relationships

In 2017, Cardi B began associating publicly with rapper Offset (born Kiari Kendrell Cephus), a member of the southern rap trio Migos. Their attraction quickly grew into romance. During Cardi B's performance at the Hot 99 Powerhouse Concert in Philadelphia on October 27, 2017, Offset proposed marriage. She accepted his offer, which caused several TV networks to begin vying for the right to broadcast the wedding.

At one point during the early part of their relationship, rumors suggested that Cardi B was "successfully hiding a baby

Kiari Kendrell Cephus, aka Offset

bump," meaning that she was pregnant with Offset's child and trying to keep it a secret. Cardi B, who has no children, and Offset (the father of two sons and a daughter from previous relationships) have denied the rumor. When another woman claimed to be pregnant with Offset's child, Cardi B, in her style, took to Instagram to defend her man and shoot down any suggestion that he was the father of the woman's child.

Musical Progress

While still dancing and making a living, Cardi B began posting on Instagram, a popular social media site. She built a following through many of the videos she posted, which were noticed and quickly spread. The activity caught the attention of VH1 and the producers of the hit show *Love & Hip Hop: New York*, as well as talent recruiters and promoters in the music industry.

Popcaan

Cardi B's performance on Shaggy's remix *Boom Boom* (along with deejay Popcaan) in November 2015 signaled the launch of her singing career. Joining the cast of *Love & Hip Hop: New York* in its sixth season in 2016 further positioned her in the limelight and brought attention to her growing success as an artist.

Cardi B found early success as an artist via social media. Her path to stardom is similar to that which was chosen by another digital music superstar, Chance the Rapper. Cardi B found that using the social media platform Instagram allowed her the freedom needed to be fully expressive and give potential audiences a hint at the tremendous talent she had in store.

Cardi B's 16.4 million followers on Instagram (iamcardib https://www.instagram.com/iamcardib/?hl=en) are nearly 200,000 more followers than the former president of the United States, Barack Obama.

Becoming Even More Recognized

Cardi B, despite the newness of her career, has put out three mixtapes so far. One of them is a compilation of her 2016 eleven-city tour promoted by KSR Group, titled UNDERESTIMATED: THE ALBUM. She has also released six single records (EPs), including her history-making number one hit *Bodak Yellow (Money Moves)*, which places her in rare company. The only other female rap artist to top *Billboard*'s Hot 100 Chart has been Lauryn Hill. Cardi B's success with *Bodak Yellow*

Cardi B's Bodak Yellow bumped Taylor Swift's Look What You Made Me Do out of Billboard's number one spot.

Ashanti

(*Money Moves*) even unseated Taylor Swift's pop hit, *Look What You Made Me Do*, to earn the number one position!

Cementing Cardi B's rise to stardom has been scoring two additional top Hot 100 Chart hits, and all of them appeared in the top ten. This includes *MotorSports*, with fellow performer of Caribbean descent (Dominican) Nicki Minaj. Cardi B's fiancée, Offset, joined in the production of *MotorSports* with his group, Migos. Her *Finesse (Remix)* with Bruno Mars was another fast-rising hit.

MotorSports peaked on *Billboard*'s Hot 100 Chart at number six, while *Finesse (Remix)* made it as high as number three. Landing three top-ten hits is not only proof of her rising stardom, it puts her in a rare circle of artists. Only the Beatles and singer Ashanti were able to score top tens on the *Billboard* Hot 100 Chart with their first three releases. Cardi B scored with *Bodak Yellow (Money Moves)*, *MotorSports*, and *No Limit*.

KSR Group

This talent management and independent record label is part of Atlantic Records. The group has Cardi B signed as part of its artists roster, along with Lil' Kim, Chris Brown, Rick Ross, LL Cool J, and Cardi B's little sister, Hennessy Carolina.

KSR Group put together the young artist's first promotional tour, Cardi B and Friends. The circuit was created to promote her and several other KSR Group artists. The musicians completed their successful, eleven-city tour in New York City at Stage 48, a club located in Manhattan, on July 29, 2016. KSR followed up on the success of the tour with the release of a mixtape on September 12, 2016, titled UNDERESTIMATED: THE ALBUM.

Her collaborative song *Heaven on My Mind*, with fellow KSR Group artist Josh X, was performed for KSR's tour and ultimately reached the *Billboard* Hot 100 Chart, peaking at number twenty-two. Cardi B's successful partnership with KSR in the early days of her career allowed her to develop her sound and her voice and enabled her to sign her first major deal with record label Atlantic Records in 2017. The move up to the "big leagues" has made her a star and an artist who is smashing chart records with every new release.

Atlantic Records

In February 2017, Cardi B accepted a multimillion-dollar deal with Atlantic Records and signed her first professional label contract. She confirmed the agreement in the summer 2017 issue of *The Fader* in a cover story titled, "Cardi B Did It Her Way." She told the publication that she had planned to remain an independent artist, but the offer was too good to let it slip by. The contract gives Cardi B serious and substantial industry backing and will open the doors to other opportunities.

Her debut single for Atlantic, *Bodak Yellow (Money Moves)*, topped the U.S. *Billboard* Hot 100 Chart for three weeks in a row, giving Atlantic a taste of what is sure to come later.

Hard Work Equals Success

From an early age, Cardi B knew that she needed to work hard for everything she wanted in life. Her early releases and efforts with KSR Group led to a deal with Atlantic Records reportedly to be for $4–$5 million. That contract resulted in the release of her number one single *Bodak Yellow (Money Moves)* and collaborations with G-Eazy (*No Limit*, which hit number four on the *Billboard* Hot 100), Migos and Nicki Minaj (*MotorSports*, a *Billboard* Hot 100 track that ranked number six), and Bruno Mars (*Finesse (Remix)*, a *Billboard* Hot 100–ranking song that reached number three).

As a rising star in the world of hip-hop and rap, she has earned her success. Before becoming an Instagram user of note and before becoming a regular cast member for two seasons on VH1's popular *Love & Hip Hop: New York* series, she was Belcalis Almanzar, working to support herself and her dreams in a Manhattan **bodega**. She has accomplished many goals in her young life so far, arriving at this point through her efforts and the achievements she has completed to realize her dreams.

Text-Dependent Questions:

❶ What is Cardi B's real birth name? What is her ethnicity?

❷ What is the name of the high school that Cardi B attended, and where is it located? Did she attend college? If so, what is the name of the school she studied at?

❸ What other performers—along with Cardi B—have had at least three songs on *Billboard*'s Hot 100 Chart?

Research Project:

Cardi B is quickly becoming one of the hottest acts in the music industry, with five songs simultaneously appearing in the top ten of *Billboard*'s R&B/Hip-Hop Songs Chart—the only female performer to reach this accomplishment since 1958, when the chart was created. What other artists have also charted five or more top-ten songs on *Billboard*'s R&B/Hip-Hop Songs Chart at the same time? This would mean holding at least five of the ten positions with their songs for a minimum of one week. Name the artist, the songs, the ranking in the top ten, and the number of weeks all five songs appeared in the top ten on this chart.

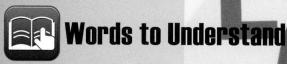
gregarious: fun-loving, over-the-top; someone who always wants to be in the company of others, or whose good times happen with others around.

hiatus: a break from an activity, or recess, for a time.

infectious: that which can be spread to others, like a disease; a friendly, happy person with a good personality who can spread their good nature and positivity to others.

leverage: to use something (such as a particular circumstance or opportunity) to achieve the best possible advantage or situation.

penchant: a habit toward or consistent ability to do the same things or same type of activities.

Chapter 3:

Making Her Way into New Industries

Venturing outside of Music

C ardi B has an out-loud, **gregarious** personality, an **infectious** laugh, and a **penchant** for having a good time. She doesn't censor herself, which is certainly part of her charm and grit. Her extraordinary personality has propelled her to the top of the music charts and placed her name on the lips of hip-hop and rap fans not only in the United States but around the world.

Fashion Moves

Acting is not the only area Cardi B is venturing into as she continues to **leverage** her success and make, as she calls them, her "money moves." Cardi B has also dipped her toes in the water of the fashion world and is eyeing it as another industry in which to make her mark. With a strong sense of personal style and the ability to dress to meet expectations for any occasion, she causes heads to turn and take notice of her fashion-forward sense in the process.

Part of Cardi B's drive to become relevant in the fashion world stems from the numerous rebuffs she received early in her career. As she was rising on Instagram as a social media star, many of the top designers and labels would not give her the opportunity to model their clothes and promote their names. So Cardi B simply adopted a different attitude toward the designers, telling *Billboard*,

> *They didn't really wanna work with me. I said to myself, 'You know what? I'm gonna buy their pieces until they wanna work with me…'*

New York Fashion Week

At the 2017 annual New York Fashion Week events—held in September each year—Cardi B came dressed to impress. Coming off the success of her number one single and high name recognition allowed her to be selected as a guest judge for British make-up artist Pat McGrath's "Mothership" Vogueing Ball, along with supermodel Naomi Campbell.

Mothership Vogueing Ball

The Mothership Vogueing Ball was a kickoff event for 2017's New York Fashion Week. It was held at the China Chalet, a dim-sum-parlor-by-day-dance-club-by-night venue located at 47 Broadway Street. The location is in the Financial District, near the site of the new World Trade Center and not far from the famous *Fearless Girl* and *Charging Bull* sculptures on Wall Street.

The event, the first of its kind, was a vehicle for the first full fashion collection of Pat McGrath (or "Mother," as she is commonly referred to). In addition to Cardi B and model Naomi Campbell, actors Tracee Ellis Ross and Teyana Taylor also served as judges.

Fenty x Puma Presentation

The skyrocketing artist showed off her style at several of the Fashion Week events, including singer Rihanna's Fenty x

The Fearless Girl *statue facing* Charging Bull *in Lower Manhattan, New York City*

Puma presentation. Cardi B gave photographers a shot of her casual and fun side as she dressed in an orange Fenty x Puma puffer jacket, blue denim shorts, and white Louis Vuitton booties to complete her ensemble. She also wore styles fashioned by designers like Christian Siriano and the famed Alexander Wang during the week.

Fashion designer Alexander Wang

Alexander Wang's After-Party

Cardi B was dressed in a black fringed netted dress (a dress that looked like netting) at this after-party, where she performed her song *Bodak Yellow (Money Moves)*. The term "after-party" refers to any get-together that takes place late into the night, usually following a different event. Alexander Wang's annual party, called "Wangfest," takes place after the main action of New York's Fashion Week.

On Camera and on Film

As she continues to rack up hits on the top of *Billboard*'s Hot 100 Chart and on the R&B/Hip-Hop Song Chart, Cardi B has ventured into the world of television and movies. Her experiences on seasons six and seven of VH1's *Love and Hip Hop: New York* series spotlighted her personality—sometimes funny, sometimes combative—and has made her a fast-rising star.

Movie Business?

According to the entertainment news reporting site TMZ, Cardi B scaled back on her touring schedule for March 2018, which they say may be an indication that she is preparing to shoot a movie. The deliberate **hiatus** will cost her about $100,000 in performance fees for the month.

Additional rumors among production people in the movie business say that the movie being discussed to highlight Cardi B's acting abilities is a comedy. The rumors further suggest that a movie like the 2017 hit *Girls Trip*—starring rapper and singer Queen Latifah, Jada Pinkett Smith, and Regina Hall—is what has been offered to Cardi B.

Actor/singer Queen Latifah on Hollywood Boulevard

Love & Hip Hop: New York

Cardi B became a part of the cast of VH1's *Love & Hip Hop: New York* series in 2015, joining the show's sixth season. As a regular cast member, she performed alongside other notable actors such as Felicia "Snoop" Pearson, who was a featured player in the HBO series *The Wire*, and rapper Remy Ma, who appeared in the 2005 animated short, *The Roaches.*

Cardi B's addition to the cast contributed a much-needed spark to the long-running series and also created a necessary level of drama and tension that was needed to sustain its ratings. She became an instant celebrity on the show, leveraging the fandom she had built during her time as a social media star on Instagram, and gave audiences glimpses of the raw, gritty, in-your-face personality that has been described as her "realness."

Cardi B appeared in thirty episodes of the show as a cast member. As her music began to become more popular and her appeal to audiences spread wider, the demands of shooting a television series while being a breakout performing star were too much. The show added her sister Hennessy to the cast, first as a guest and calming influence for Cardi B, toward the end of the sixth season. But as Cardi B's decision to leave the show was becoming obvious, Hennessy became a regular part of the show in place of her sister.

As Cardi B's career grew and more opportunities to create and perform came her way, she finally revealed her final show would be in December 2016. The announcement was made via a post she put up live on her Instagram account. She told her fans that in order to get serious about becoming a rapper, she needed to focus more on her music and spend less time on television.

Regarding her two seasons on the popular reality show, Cardi B said,

> *I don't want people to think I became a rapper because I was on* Love & Hip Hop [New York]. *There are a couple of songs that are on my mixtape [GBM* VOL.1] *that I been did before* Love & Hip Hop—*it just wasn't completely perfect. It wasn't completely perfect and everything takes time. It took me like a year to complete the mixtape. Everything I do, it takes a lot of time for me to do it because only the best sells, you know? If you want people to take you seriously, you gotta do the best.*

Other TV Shows and Appearances

In addition to Cardi B's two seasons on VH1's *Love & Hip Hop: New York*, she has made appearances on a variety of programs, mainly as a music performer. The list of additional shows that she has received a credit for include the following.

Kocktails with Khloé

April 06, 2016

Khloé Kardashian *(Keeping up with the Kardashians)* invited Cardi B for tea, along with Tisha Campbell Martin, Jeannie Mai, Ta'Rhonda Jones, and James Maslow. During the program, they discussed

Khloé Kardashian

current news, gossip, and the events going on in each of the celebrity's lives.

Questions: Election Special Hosted by Cardi B!
September 05, 2016

Cardi B appeared on an election-year special for the video blog *WSHH* titled *Questions: Election Special*. "WSHH" stands for WorldStarHipHop. The internet-based video blog was founded in 2005 and is dedicated to fans of hip-hop music. This particular program took a look at the issues and candidates in the 2016 U.S. presidential election.

Hip Hop Squares

This show was created for the VH1 network by rapper Ice Cube. The program, a clever imitation of the classic game show *Hollywood Squares*, features panelists arranged in three rows of stacked boxes of three, like a tic-tac-toe game. Contestants are asked questions, and they select one as being true from the answers given by three chosen panelists. If the answer from the selected panelist is really true, an "X" is lit up in that panelist's box. The contestant who scores a tic-tac-toe wins the game.

Cardi B appeared as a panelist on *Hip Hop Squares* on three different shows in 2017:

- March 13, 2017: Contestants were Ray J vs. Princess Love
- April 03, 2017: Contestants were Jessica White vs. Joe Budden
- October 02, 2017: Contestants were Trina vs. Dreezy

The Wendy Williams Show

July 18, 2017

Cardi B appeared as the musical guest on *The Wendy Williams Show* on July 18, 2017. She performed her hit song *Bodak Yellow (Money Moves)* for the audience, and comedian Mario Cantone was also a guest.

The Tonight Show Starring Jimmy Fallon

September 26, 2017

The musical guest on Jimmy Fallon's *The Tonight Show* on this date was Cardi B. She performed the song *No Limit* with G-Eazy. The show also featured actors Kate Winslet and Milo Ventimiglia from the NBC hit show, *This Is Us*.

December 20, 2017

Cardi B appeared again on the show in December, along with actor Christoph Waltz, comedian Elizabeth Greer "Beanie" Feldstein, and singer Erykah Badu. Cardi B was a guest this time and didn't perform. She and host Jimmy Fallon discussed her successful 2017.

Scan here to watch Cardi B perform her hit song *Bodak Yellow (Money Moves)* for the audience of *The Wendy Williams Show*

Scan here
to watch
Cardi B begin
her interview
with host
Jimmy Fallon of
The Tonight Show
on a December
2017 taping of
the show

Jimmy Kimmel Live!
October 18, 2017

Cardi B performed her hit song *Bodak Yellow (Money Moves)* for *Jimmy Kimmel Live!* on this episode. The show also featured an interview with shock jock Howard Stern, and composer Paul Shaffer sat in with Jimmy Kimmel's house band, Cleto and the Cletones.

The band takes its name from its leader, saxophonist Cleto Escobedo III, a Las Vegas neighbor of the host, Jimmy Kimmel. Escobedo has played alongside artists such as Paula Abdul, Marc Anthony, and Philip Bailey, formerly of Earth, Wind & Fire.

Access Hollywood
December 14, 2017

As a rising hip-hop star, Cardi B was interviewed in the season twenty-two episode of *Access Hollywood*. In the interview, she provided tips and advice on dating, what to do to keep romance alive, and how to respond when first getting someone's number.

Celebrity Page

January 17, 2018

Cardi B appeared in episode eighty-nine of the third season. This celebrity entertainment news, gossip, and fashion show, hosted by Sonia Isabelle and Jaymes Vaughan, airs on the Reelz Channel.

Commercials and Endorsements

Cardi B hasn't stopped making money moves since her star began rising, but she has had a difficult time attracting

Scan here to watch Cardi B as she performs her hit song *Bodak Yellow (Money Moves)* for the audience of *Jimmy Kimmel Live!* in October 2017

attention from fashion designers and brand owners. Even designer Christian Louboutin—whose pale green dress Cardi B displayed during her support for Rihanna's annual Fashion Week charitable event, the Diamond Ball—was not familiar with her work as a rapper and was unsure about how to describe the type of work she does.

Steve Madden

A signed endorsement deal for Steve Madden shoes in 2017 provides Cardi B with a way to make a fashion statement with her new shoe collection. The partnership is in line with her style,

Scan the code here to watch Cardi B in her first acting commercial, where she also provides the voice-over for a local New York City small business

character, and personality and definitely supports the money moves she has been making.

The deal marks a first for Cardi B, as she has been looking for a way to popularize her personal style and sense of fashion. It will include a curated collection of designer sunglasses and boots and is scheduled to feature thigh-high boots matching the style and expressive nature of their namesake, Cardi B. Yellow-lensed sunglasses are expected to sell for $36, and on the high end, a pair of white platform boots will retail for around $230. In addition to the merchandise, Cardi B will be featured in a sponsored video series called *Daily Tips with Cardi B*.

Pawn Rite

As Cardi B waits to grab the attention of more fashion houses and other big-time advertisers, she took advantage of a lull in her schedule to shoot a tongue-in-cheek advertising spot for a local pawnshop chain in Brooklyn called Pawn Rite. The one-minute ad, which can be seen online, shows Cardi B at a fancy restaurant facing a $47,000 dinner bill with her "date," who appears to have run out of money.

Cardi B provides the voice-over for the commercial, telling viewers the types of items that can be pawned for cash at any of Pawn Rite's three New York City locations.

Elle

Cardi B shot a video spot for the magazine *Elle*, speaking on the subject of beauty and feeling beautiful. The one-and-a-half-minute spot is an honest monologue that Cardi B offers to the camera—and the viewers—giving a glimpse into a softer, toned-down image (in contrast to her performing persona or characterization on *Love & Hip Hop: New York*).

Award Shows Beginning to Take Notice

Cardi B has been nominated for nineteen awards and has been the recipient of six of them since first appearing on the scene in 2015, including two Grammy nominations in 2018 for her hit song *Bodak Yellow (Money Moves)*. Here is a listing of the awards Cardi B has won or been nominated for during her career so far.

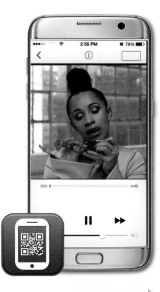

Scan the code here to watch Cardi B offer her personal beauty tips and give her general opinion on what makes her feel and look beautiful

Award Nominations

BET Awards

Best New Artist | Nominated in 2017

Best Female Hip-Hop Artist | Nominated in 2017

BET Hip-Hop Awards

Single of the Year—*Bodak Yellow (Money Moves)* | Won in 2017

Best New Hip-Hop Artist | Won in 2017

Hustler of the Year | Won in 2017

Made-You-Look Award (Best Hip-Hop Style) | Won in 2017

Best Mixtape—GBM, Vol:2 | Won in 2017

Best Hip-Hop Video—*Bodak Yellow (Money Moves)* | Nominated in 2017

Impact Track—*Bodak Yellow (Money Moves)* | Nominated in 2017

Hot Ticket Performer | Nominated in 2017

MVP of the Year | Nominated in 2017

Grammy Awards

Best Rap Performance—*Bodak Yellow (Money Moves)* | Nominated in 2018

Best Rap Song—*Bodak Yellow (Money Moves)* | Nominated in 2018

iHeartRadio Music Awards

Best New Hip-Hop Artist | Nominated in 2018

Hip-Hop Song of the Year—*Bodak Yellow (Money Moves)* | Nominated in 2018

Best Lyrics—*Bodak Yellow (Money Moves)* | Nominated in 2018

Best Music Video—*Bodak Yellow (Money Moves)* | Nominated in 2018

Mobo Awards

Best International Act—Cardi B | Nominated in 2017

Soul Train Music Awards

Rhythm & Bars Award—*Bodak Yellow (Money Moves)* | Won in 2017

Remy Ma appeared as one of the cast of actors on the show Love & Hip Hop: New York, along with Cardi B

Text-Dependent Questions:

❶ Who did Cardi B perform with during a September 26, 2017, airing of *The Tonight Show with Jimmy Fallon*? What song did they perform?

❷ What did Cardi B do during her October 18, 2017, appearance on the *Jimmy Kimmel Live!* show?

❸ What is the name of the tic-tac-toe-style show that Cardi B made three appearances on as a panelist?

Research Project:

Cardi B used her experience as a member of the cast of VH1's *Love & Hip Hop: New York* as a stepping-stone to stardom as a female rap artist. She appeared on the show as part of a group of actors that included Remy Ma, who went on to have a hugely successful career as a rapper, and Felicia Pearson, a rapper from Baltimore who also worked as an actress and had a credited role on the acclaimed HBO show *The Wire* (as Snoop). Name three other hip-hop/rap stars who first appeared on a television show and used their fame to launch a music career. (Hint: One performer appeared on a successful NBC show and is the creator of a second show for the FX Network.)

Words to Understand

feisty: someone who is testy, restless; someone struggling or lashing out against others or something.

forum: an outlet for expressing views or opinions to others, such as a stage, lecture, classroom, online blog, and so on.

garner: bring focus or attention to yourself or an issue of concern or importance.

influencer: someone who has the ability to bring others forward or create a large group of supporters and have influence over their views and opinions.

#MeToo: a social media hashtag campaign that started on Twitter; used by survivors of sexual assault and harassment to raise awareness and highlight how common it is.

Chapter 4

Cardi B—Building a Brand

Social Media Presence

Cardi B began **garnering** attention through her use of the social media site Instagram. Glimpses of her personality and wild, **feisty** side began to show on the account, which stimulated interest in her as an artist and public figure.

She has more than 16.4 million followers worldwide and is seen as a social media **influencer**. This role makes a tremendous platform available to her to promote her latest projects, reach out to fans, and spotlight her image. Cardi B's use of social media has provided her with a fantastic **forum** and an important outlet for her views, opinions, and interaction with the public.

By way of comparison, former president Barack Obama has 16.2 million followers on his Instagram

Former president Barack Obama

account. Although Cardi B has more fans than the former president, her presence on the social media site is still below the top ten Instagram influencers. Actor Selena Gomez tops the list for the most number of fans, with 130 million Instagram followers worldwide. Taylor Swift—whom Cardi B unseated at the number one spot on *Billboard*'s Hot 100 Chart—has 104 million followers, putting her at number six on the list of celebrities with the most admirers.

Selena Gomez

Cardi B also uses Twitter and Facebook and has large followings on both. Her handle on Twitter, where she has 2.23 million followers, is @imcardib (https://twitter.com/iamcardib). On Facebook, her username is almost identical—Iamcardib—and she can be found at https://www.facebook.com/IamCardiB/ with her 3.7 million fans.

It doesn't appear that Cardi B has taken to Snapchat quite yet. That domain is currently dominated by record producer and music executive/deejay DJ Khaled.

Streaming Availability

Cardi B uses different digital platforms and internet radio services to make her music available to fans. Included in these platforms are each of the major music-streaming and internet radio services—Spotify, iTunes, Apple Music, Pandora, and Google Music—and channels on Last.fm, Slacker Radio, and iHeartRadio. Below is a list of the different ways you can listen to Cardi B's music online through a favorite internet radio or streaming-music service.

Cardi B Internet Radio Stations

Amazon Music
Apple Music
Google Play
iHeart Radio
Last.fm
Pandora
Slacker Radio
Spotify

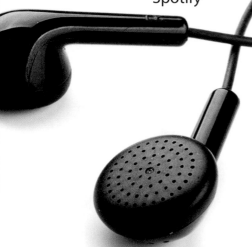

Cardi B Digital Music Platforms

DatPiff.com
iTunes
SoundCloud
YouTube

Cardi B: Feminist Icon

When you get past some of the lyrics in her hit song *Bodak Yellow (Money Moves)*, "you find a deeper hidden meaning in the message of feminism" that Cardi B encourages in her audiences, especially young girls. Her breakout track seems to be a retelling of her life as a dancer before becoming a star on Instagram, but a closer examination reveals more than that.

In one line in the song, she refers to herself as "the boss." Using this adjective is an expression of how Cardi B has gone from being just a worker to someone in control of her fate and in charge of her own destiny. The money moves she has made have allowed her to sign deals and improve her financial situation. They have also left her and her music positioned in a way that has made her very successful in a very short amount of time. It is an impressive accomplishment for any artist to land one top-ten song on *Billboard*'s Hot 100 Chart. But to do so with so many different songs—and to have three of them on the chart at the same time— places her within a unique circle of professionals.

Cardi B's star has risen fast and steadily, and her attitude of control

Janet Jackson

makes her presence in the world of
music and hip-hop more relevant for
young girls today. This is especially
true when considering issues such
as the **#MeToo** campaign against
harassment and aggression. Even a
megastar like Janet Jackson took the
time to pay tribute to Cardi B during
a 2017 concert. She danced to a clip
from Cardi B's *Bodak Yellow (Money
Moves)* during a show in September.
It was one of the fifty-six scheduled
stops on Janet's State of the World
Tour, produced by Live Nation.

Scan the code here to watch
music legend Janet Jackson
dance to *Bodak Yellow (Money
Moves)*, Cardi B's Top 100 hit

The idea that Cardi B represents a
new sense of feminism in the world
of rap for female artists stems from
the fact that she has risen to the
top largely on the strength of her own efforts. Lauryn Hill, who
preceded her to the top of *Billboard*'s Hot 100 Chart twenty years
ago, was with the group The Fugees, which helped elevate her
toward eventual solo success. More contemporary artists like Lil'
Kim, Iggy Azalea, Nicki Minaj, and Eve all relied on the support of
male counterparts—where Cardi B relied on Cardi B.

For Nicki Minaj, there was Lil Wayne. For Eve, rapper DMX
supported her initial work. Lil' Kim succeeded through the
mentorship of Biggie Smalls, and for Iggy, there was T.I. Not only
was this not the case for Cardi B, but her rise to the top now means

that male performers are looking to latch on to her success and collaborate with her in order to catch some of the magic taking her to higher ground.

Her success on the charts as an out-the-box, break-the-mold performer is tearing down long-held opinions about how female rappers should look and act. She is giving hope to the next generation of performers that they will not need to seek the assistance of a male counterpart to become successful. Cardi B shows them that they can become successful in their own right, based on the strength of their hard work, effort, and talent.

Lil Wayne performs at Sleep Train Amphitheater in Chula Vista, CA

Text-Dependent Questions:

❶ How many Twitter followers does Cardi B have?

❷ What megastar singer performed dance moves to Cardi B's *Bodak Yellow (Money Moves)* during a concert appearance in 2017?

❸ What was the reported amount of the deal that Cardi B signed with Atlantic Records?

Research Project:

Cardi B's use of social media has allowed her to reach her fans in a way that would not have been possible ten or twenty years ago. The interest she created through her online interactions is what helped her transition from worker to boss, moving from appearing on the show *Love & Hip Hop: New York* to becoming a featured performer for KSR Group to signing her first major recording deal with Atlantic Records. As it appears that more and more young artists are creating buzz for themselves through social media, name the top three hip-hop and rap artists on each of the following platforms (by number of likes or followers): Instagram, Twitter, Facebook, and Snapchat. Name the artist, the number of followers (or likes), and the amount of time they have had their account on the respective platform.

Words to Understand

groundbreaking: something new, innovative, trendsetting.

legacy: something of value left behind by a person after she has moved on; a tangible item inherited, a mark or accomplishments in a field, or a will are forms of legacies that people create.

ravaged: attacked, mauled, or set upon by another.

viral: a social media post that spreads quickly and is seen by many people in a short period of time.

Chapter 5

Using Fame to Give Back to the Community

Tidal X 2017 Benefit Concert

The year 2017 was noted as the one of the deadliest Atlantic Ocean hurricane seasons, tied with the year 1936 for number five. Seventeen named storms—including six rated as a category three or higher—**ravaged** the Caribbean, including the U.S. territory of Puerto Rico and the Gulf of Mexico. In addition, Hurricane Harvey came ashore in the Houston, Texas, area during August 17–September 3, 2017.

The hurricane season began on June 01 and came to a close on November 30, 2017. Including all the storms during the season, they caused more than $290 billion in damage, and many people died in Honduras, the Bahamas, Puerto Rico, and the southern United States, including Texas and Florida. The actual number of deaths is not yet known.

USA TODAY *with Hurricane Maria breaking news*

There were many charity events organized in the fall of 2017 to raise money for relief efforts in support of the areas affected by the storms and the lives that were impacted. One of the largest efforts was a social media appeal made by J. J. Watt, a Houston Texans defensive end and National Football League star. Wanting to raise $200,000 in support of the Houston-area victims of the storm, the campaign quickly went **viral** and resulted in $37 million raised.

One benefit concert, organized by the global music and entertainment platform Tidal, was held in Brooklyn, New York, on October 17, 2017, at the Barclays Center. The concert, third in an annual series, was headlined by Jay-Z. Cardi B participated in the benefit concert as a performer and lent her talents to this worthwhile charitable cause. Other artists performing at the event included Stevie Wonder, Jennifer Lopez, and DJ Khaled.

Fast Fact 3:

Tidal X—This program connects artists and their fans in unique ways—not just concerts, but meet-and-greets, autograph-signing events, ticket giveaways, and exclusive live shows. The annual Tidal X charity concert, which is streamed live via the Tidal entertainment platform, raises funds for various charities. In 2015, Tidal X: 1020 (October 20) benefited charities "dedicated to advancing positive community relations and effecting systemic change for the development and sustainability of just societies." Tidal X: 1015 (October 15) in 2016 was a four-hour event that benefited several nonprofit organizations dedicated to improving education.

The funds collected from the 2017 Tidal X benefit were disbursed to organizations that were providing relief efforts in the United States, including Puerto Rico, which was devastated by the effects of Hurricane Maria. Charities that received monies included the Greater Houston Community Foundation, Global Giving, and Direct Relief.

Rihanna's Diamond Ball

Cardi B was spotted at several events during New York's annual Fashion Week events in 2017. One of the celebrations that she attended, providing her support, was Rihanna's Diamond Ball. The 2017 Diamond Ball took place on September 15 and was the third annual in a series of balls hosted by singer Rihanna to raise money to provide for worthy causes.

Scan the code here to watch Cardi B's performance at the 2017 Tidal X concert at Brooklyn's Barclays Center for victims of that year's Atlantic hurricane season

Fast Fact 4:

The Diamond Ball, started during Fashion Week in 2015, increases awareness and attention to issues that Rihanna is concerned about. Through their attendance and participation, other artists offer their support and fund-raising skills to assist her. Rihanna, who is an ambassador for the Global Partnership for Education for Global Citizen, used the ball in 2017 to provide funds for the Clara Lionel Foundation.

Established by Rihanna in 2012 in honor of her grandparents, Clara and Lionel Braithwaite, the Clara Lionel Foundation is dedicated to providing money to global charities that are involved in **groundbreaking** opportunities for education. The organization also advocates on behalf of young people in order to improve their lives.

Rihanna

The 2017 Diamond Ball was well attended by nearly every A-list entertainer, including comedian Dave Chappelle, who delivered a monologue praising Rihanna's foundation. Chappelle also paid $180,000 in an auction for an original Retna painting. It was donated to the function by the well-known American street artist himself, and the proceeds of that auction were added to the more than $3 million raised during the evening.

Cardi B proudly gave her support to the charitable event, appearing at the ball in a pale green Christian Siriano gown. The gown was so poufy that it required Cardi B to travel in the trunk of her SUV as she was transported to the event's venue! The dress also required the assistance of four handlers in order to put Cardi B comfortably into the vehicle and assist her out. Apparently, it was no trouble for Cardi B to provide her support for the worthwhile charity.

The restaurant hosting the event, Cipriani Wall Street in New York City, is located in the historic building housing the New York Merchants Exchange, New York Stock Exchange, and U.S. Customs House.

Cardi B's Diamond Ball appearance occurred among a who's who list of stars arriving at Cipriani's for the event. In addition to Dave Chappelle and Cardi B, attendees also included Leo DiCaprio, Kendrick Lamar, Lil' Kim, Yo Gotti, and, of course, Jay-Z and Beyoncé.

Support for Colin Kaepernick

After her performance at the 2017 MTV Video Music Awards preshow, Cardi B acknowledged her support for former San Francisco 49ers quarterback Colin Kaepernick. She announced to her fans and those who came to hear her perform her hit song, *Bodak Yellow (Money Moves)*: "Colin Kaepernick, as long as you kneel with us, we're gonna be standing for you."

Colin Kaepernick

The shout-out, delivered after her song and before her introduction for Demi Lovato, was a reference to Kaepernick's decision to kneel before the start of games in the 2016 National Football League (NFL) season during the singing of the U.S. national anthem. The "kneel down protest," as it came to be known, was designed to bring focus and attention to the issue of police brutality against communities of color and the need for a dialogue to take place in order to stop the rise in the deaths of young black men at the hands of law enforcement officers.

Colin Kaepernick's stance cost him his job in the NFL but has made him a culturally popular voice for civil rights. He has turned this role into an opportunity to raise awareness and funds for causes that support his view, including a gift of $30,000 to fellow rapper and admirer of Cardi B's artistry, J. Cole of Roc Nation (Jay-Z's management group), and his charity, the Dreamville Foundation.

Fast Fact 5:

J. Cole messaged Cardi B directly in support of her upcoming album project in September 2017. The shared tweet provided gentle encouragement and support and was received very well by Cardi B. ""Is this real :') Son my heart is smiling," she responded to the Born Sinner artist (J. Cole's second studio album) on Twitter. "Well who am I not to take J Cole advice?"

Cardi B has subsequently reiterated her support for Colin Kaepernick. During a Super Bowl LII pregame appearance, she was asked when she would appear in the event's famous halftime show. In a video recorded by TMZ, she responded, "When they hire Colin Kaepernick back."

Conclusion

Cardi B's life began in the Highbridge neighborhood of the Bronx in New York City. Born of immigrant parents—a Dominican father and mother from Trinidad—she was determined to support herself, always dreaming of a better life. Nothing was handed to her, but through perseverance, hard work, and a drive to become successful, she found herself facing different opportunities. Managing them successfully has put her in the envied position she is in today.

Trinidad is famous for its lovely, cobblestone streets and pastel-coloured houses with elaborate wrought-iron grills

She is the first female rapper in twenty years to reach the top of the *Billboard* Hot 100 Chart with her number one song *Bodak Yellow (Money Moves)*. She has become a social media influencer and, through her Instagram account, caught the attention of the right people who helped her career along. A successful eleven-day tour in July 2016 gave her a taste of the success yet to come.

Since then, Cardi B has accepted a multimillion-dollar contract with Atlantic Records, one of her biggest money moves to date. Signing with a major record label has increased her exposure and allowed her to become the star she is today. Very few artists have established themselves as a chart-making hit machine like Cardi B has. Within a short time, she finds herself sitting on the top of the hip-hop and rap mountain.

As Cardi B continues to grow and mature, she will be able to see the potential of her influence on her young fans, especially girls who look up to her. The stage will be a platform for her form of feminism, changing mindsets from workers to bosses and encouraging women to take control of their own futures. She can take advantage of the opportunity to be a positive influence for change, paving the way for other women to be successful in whatever they choose to do.

Cardi B may be a little crude and rough around the edges, but she is also full of personality and talent. Her energy and influence will leave a **legacy** long after she leaves the business. The question is, with only a few years under her belt, how much further will her star rise and what else will she be able to accomplish as a history-making performer? Only time will tell how great Cardi B will become.

Text-Dependent Questions:

❶ What performer provided a monologue at Rihanna's 2017 Diamond Ball event that Cardi B attended on September 15, 2017? How much money was raised by the event?

❷ What was the name of the benefit concert that Cardi B performed at in Brooklyn at the Barclays Center on October 17, 2017, to help those people who were victims of the 2017 hurricane season?

❸ How many people did it take to help Cardi B with the dress she chose to wear for Rihanna's Diamond Ball? What is the name of the designer of her ball dress?

Research Project:

Cardi B has supported several personal causes of her fellow performers. In 2017 alone, she attended Rihanna's Diamond Ball—assisting the singer in raising money on behalf of young people around the world—and performed at an October benefit concert to raise money for hurricane victims in the Caribbean and eastern and southern United States. Who are three of the largest hip-hop/rap stars that raise funds on behalf of a cause or for a specific community need (such as education, housing, prison reform, etc.)? Name the artist, the amount of money the artist raised in 2017, and the type of charitable activity that was involved—such as a ball or gala, dinner, celebrity sport tournament, benefit concert, or a similar type of event.

Series Glossary of Key Terms

A&R: an abbreviation that stands for Artists and Repertoire, which is a record company department responsible for the recruitment and development of talent; similar to a talent scout for sports.

ambient: a musical style that relies on electronic sounds, gentle music, and the lack of a regular beat to create a relaxed mood for the listener.

brand: a particular product or a characteristic that serves to identify a particular product; a brand name is one having a well-known and usually highly regarded or marketable word or phrase.

cameo: also called a cameo role; a minor part played by a prominent performer in a single scene of a motion picture or a television show.

choreography: the art of planning and arranging the movements, steps, and patterns of dancers.

collaboration: a product created by working with someone else; combining individual talents.

debut: a first public appearance on a stage, on television, or so on, or the beginning of a profession or career; the first appearance of something, like a new product.

deejay (DJ): a slang term for a person who spins vinyl records on a turntable; aka a disc jockey.

demo: a recording of a new song, or of one performed by an unknown singer or group, distributed to disc jockeys, recording companies, and the like, to demonstrate the merits of the song or performer.

dubbed: something that is named or given a new name or title; in movies, when the actors' voices have been replaced with those of different performers speaking another language; in music, transfer or copying of previously recorded audio material from one medium to another.

endorsement: money earned from a product recommendation, typically by a celebrity, athlete, or other public figure.

entrepreneur: a person who organizes and manages any enterprise, especially a business, usually with considerable initiative and at financial risk.

falsetto: a man singing in an unnaturally high voice, accomplished by creating a vibration at the very edge of the vocal chords.

genre: a subgroup or category within a classification, typically associated with works of art, such as music or literature.

hone, honing: sharpening or refining a set of skills necessary to achieve success or perform a specific task.

icon: a symbol that represents something, such as a team, a religious person, a location, or an idea.

innovation: the introduction of something new or different; a brand-new feature or upgrade to an existing idea, method, or item.

instrumental: serving as a crucial means, agent, or tool; of, relating to, or done with an instrument or tool.

jingle: a short verse, tune, or slogan used in advertising to make a product easily remembered.

mogul: someone considered to be very important, powerful, and in charge; a term usually associated with heads of businesses in the television, movie studio, or recording industries.

performing arts: skills that require public performance, as acting, singing, or dancing.

philanthropy: goodwill to fellow members of the human race; an active effort to promote human welfare.

public relations: the activity or job of providing information about a particular person or organization to the public so that people will regard that person or organization in a favorable way.

sampler: a digital or electronic musical instrument, related to a synthesizer, that uses samples, or sound recordings, of real instruments (trumpet, violin, piano, etc.) mixed with excerpts of recorded songs and other interesting sounds (sirens, ocean waves, construction noises, car horns, etc.) that are stored digitally and can be replayed by a triggering device, like a sequencer, electronic drums, or a MIDI keyboard.

single: a music recording having two or more tracks that is shorter than an album, EP, or LP; also, a song that is particularly popular, independent of other songs on the same album or by the same artist.

Further Reading

Abrams, Howie. *Hip-Hop Alphabet.* New York: Lesser Gods, 2017.

Bradley, Adam. *Book of Rhymes: The Poetics of Hip Hop.* New York: Basic Books, 2017.

Clark, Lamont. *MCs: A Children's Guide to the Origins of Hip Hop.* Washington, DC: 70 West Press, 2013.

D, Chuck. *Chuck D Presents This Day in Rap and Hip-Hop History.* Philadelphia: Running Press, 2017.

Earl, C. F. *Hip Hop: A Short History.* New York: Simon and Schuster, 2014.

Morse, Eric, and George Nelson. *What Is Hip-Hop?* Brooklyn, NY: Akashic Books, 2017.

Pough, Gwendolyn D. *Check It While I Wreck It: Black Womanhood, Hip-Hop Culture, and the Public Sphere.* Boston: Northeastern University Press, 2015.

Semtex, DJ. *Hip Hop Raised Me.* New York: Thames & Hudson, 2016.

Internet Resources

www.billboard.com
The official website for *Billboard* magazine with information about chart rankings for musical artists from different musical genres.

thesource.com
The official website for *The Source* magazine, providing topical news and information about the world of hip-hop, rap, and the music industry.

www.vibe.com
The official *Vibe* magazine site, a source of news and information about music celebrities in rap and hip-hop.

www.vh1.com
The official website for VH1.

Educational Video Links

Chapter 1 :
http://x-qr.net/1F5L
http://x-qr.net/1FmT
http://x-qr.net/1Cto
http://x-qr.net/1Dr8
http://x-qr.net/1EeM
http://x-qr.net/1EjA
http://x-qr.net/1FZZ
http://x-qr.net/1Eog
http://x-qr.net/1DLJ
http://x-qr.net/1FPK

Chapter 3:
http://x-qr.net/1DDR
http://x-qr.net/1DPg
http://x-qr.net/1Hsc
http://x-qr.net/1DyW
http://x-qr.net/1FYL

Chapter 4:
http://x-qr.net/1DoB

Chapter 5:
http://x-qr.net/1Fix

Citations

"... she received one of the best offers in her young career ..." by Sofiya Ballin. Ballin, Sofiya. "Cardi B Gets Engaged at Power 99's Powerhouse Concert in Philly." Philly.com. October 28, 2017.

"... difficult to continue her studies ..." by Rawiya Kameir. Kameir, Rawiya. "Cardi B's So-Called Life: The Former _____ from the Bronx Turned Her Instagram Account into a Career. Now She Just Wants to Take Care of Her Family." *The Fader*. February 29, 2016.

"They didn't really wanna work with me ..." by Cardi B. Blais Billie, Braudie. "Cardi B Opens Up about Being Rejected by Fashion Designers." Billboard.com. April 22, 2017.

"... realness ..." by Braudie Blais Billie. Blais Billie, "Cardi B Opens Up ..." 2017.

"I don't want people to think ..." by Cardi B. Thompson, Desire. "Cardi B Announces Departure from 'Love & Hip Hop New York.'" *Vibe*. December 29, 2016.

"... you find a deeper hidden meaning in the message of feminism ..." by Hiram Lee. Lee, Hiram. "Rapper Cardi B ('Bodak Yellow') celebrated as a feminist icon." WSWS.org. October 09, 2017.

"... dedicated to advancing positive community relations ..." by Fabiola Antunes. Antunes, Fabiola. "TIDAL X: 10/20 Benefit Charity Concert." Afrossip.com. September 30, 2015.

"Colin Kaepernick, as long as you kneel ..." by Cardi B. NBC Sports Bay Area staff. "Cardi B Shouts Out Colin Kaepernick during 2017 VMAs." NBCSports.com. August 27, 2017.

"Is this real :') ..." by Cardi B. Martinez, Jose. "Cardi B Says Her 'Heart Is Smiling' After J. Cole Gives Her Advice on Twitter." Complex.com. September 24, 2017.

"Well who am I ..." by Cardi B. Martinez, "Cardi B Says ..." 2017.

"When they hire Colin Kaepernick back," by Cardi B. Hull, Caleb. "Cardi B Is Holding Her Future Super Bowl Performance Hostage, and It Has Everything to Do with Kaepernick." *Independent Journal Review*. February 04, 2018.

Photo Credits

Chapter 1:
ID 25685499 © Sbukley | Dreamstime
ID 5849160 © Claudiodivizia | Dreamstime
ID 26355526 © Sbukley | Dreamstime
ID 35519544 © Sbukley | Dreamstime
ID 62019966 © Ryan Deberardinis | Dreamstime
ID 98817813 © Starstock | Dreamstime
ID 14315060320 | Flickr | ©Eddy Rissling for The
Come Up Show
ID 4337304450 | Flickr | © Marcello Russo
ID: 668890132 © By Arturo Holmes | Shutterstock
ID: 741027814 © By JStone | Shutterstock
CC-BY-SA-3.0-DE © Emha / Wikimedia Commons
Juicy_J_2014_February.jpg © By Active Magazine |
Wikimedia Commons
Nawlage_&_Cardi_B.jpg © Solace Agenda |
Wikimedia Commons
Borough_of_Manhattan_Comm_College.JPG ©
MegsCommons | Wikimedia Commons

Chapter 2:
ID 9561907 © Wanderlust | Dreamstime
ID 44488321 © Tom Wang | Dreamstime
ID 55801530 © Starstock | Dreamstime
ID 108310322 © Ivetalacane | Dreamstime
ID: 772333387 © By lev radin | Shutterstock

Chapter 3:
ID 27559790 © Roystudio | Dreamstime
ID 34073910 © Little_prince | Dreamstime
ID 25007936 © Featureflash | Dreamstime
ID 25274871 © Carrienelson1 | Dreamstime
ID 25588387 © Featureflash | Dreamstime

ID 44799632 © Palinchak | Dreamstime
ID 46068486 © Jaguarps | Dreamstime
ID 70587360 © Laurence Agron | Dreamstime
ID: 730276861 © By Jamie Lamor Thompson |
Shutterstock

Chapter 4:
ID 18256756 © Viacheslav Krisanov | Dreamstime
ID 21036807 © Randy Miramontez | Dreamstime
ID 32457124 © Sbukley | Dreamstime

Chapter 5:
ID 29744363 © Filtv | Dreamstime
ID 30571463 © Carrienelson1 | Dreamstime
ID 100499951 © Ifeelstock | Dreamstime
ID 103623464 © Andre DurÃo | Dreamstime
ID: 741027946© By JStone | Shutterstock
ID: 1022659657 © By lev radin | Shutterstock
J. Cole.jpg © Kirstenmgreene | Wikimedia
Commons

Index

Index

Index

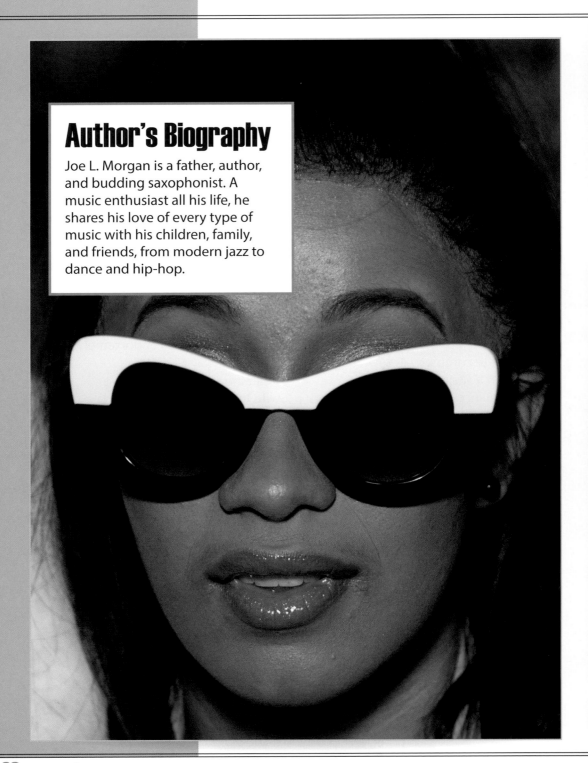

Author's Biography

Joe L. Morgan is a father, author, and budding saxophonist. A music enthusiast all his life, he shares his love of every type of music with his children, family, and friends, from modern jazz to dance and hip-hop.